A Portrait of Perfection: Blessed Descriptions of the Best of Creation

A Portrait of

Perfection:

Blessed Descriptions of the Best of Creation

Part One

Al-'Allāmah **Imam Ghiyāth al-Dīn** ibn al-'Āqūlī

Translated by

DR MOHAMMED LUQMAAN KAGEE

Translated by Dr Mohammed Luqmaan Kagee

Please treat this book with respect because it contains holy verses from the noble *Qur'ān*.

Inquiries concerning reproduction outside those terms should be sent to: Darul Latif Networks

Western Cape, South Africa

info@darallatif.net

www.darallatif.net

ISBN: 978-0-6397-8466-3

Dedication

This book is dedicated to:

Sayyidunā Muḥammad *Rasūlullāh* , the best of all creation, the seal of all Prophets, the mercy to all the worlds, the most beloved of Allāh, and our beloved Prophet.

تَاللهِ مَا حَمَلَتْ أُنْثَى وَلاَ وَضَعَتْ ... مِثْلَ الرَّسُوْلِ نَبِيِّ الْأُمَّةِ الْهَادِيْ

وَلاَ بَرَا اللهُ خَلْقًا مِنْ بَرِيَّتِهِ ... أَوْفَى بِذِمَّةِ جَارٍ أَوْ بِمِيْعَادِ

مَنْ الَّذِيْ كَانَ فِيْنَا يُسْتَضَاءُ بِهِ ... مُبَارَكَ الْأَمْرِ ذَا عَدْلٍ وَإِرْشَادِ

مُصَدِّقًا لِلنَّبِيِّيْنَ الْأُلَى سَلَفُوْا ... وَأَبْذَلَ النَّاسِ لِلْمَعْرُوْفِ لِلْجَادِيْ

By Allāh, no female has ever carried in its womb nor given birth to someone like the noble Messenger, the Prophet that guided his *ummah*. Nor has Allāh created amongst His entire creation, someone more loyal with a neighbour's rights or with a promise. Who was the one amongst us that gave us light? He is blessed in all his affairs and is one of justice and leadership. He is a confirmation for the Prophets that came before him, and he is the most generous of people when doing favours, or in giving to others.[1]

Acknowledgements

First and foremost, I offer my deepest and most sincere gratitude to Allāh , the Creator. Secondly, I send choicest peace and salutations upon our beloved Prophet, *Sayyidunā* Muḥammad , and offer him my gratitude for teaching Islam to us.

I would further, like to express my gratitude and appreciation to the following people:

- My parents, Goolam Sabier and Zainab Kagee;
- My wife, Gulshan, and son, Muhammad Usayd;
- My revered *Pir-o-Murshid* Shāh Mohamed Saied Soofie;
- Moulana Goolam Kutboodien Kagee, for proofreading;
- Shāh Abdul-Aziz Soofie of Durban;
- Dr. Shabeer Ahmed Kagee for his support;
- Shaykh Ḥāfiẓ Masood Ahmed Kagee;
- Moulana Goolam Muhammad Soofie of Durban;
- Moulana Muhammad Farouq Soofie of Durban for proofreading;

- Moulana Muhammad Ebrahim Soofie for his input regarding the title;
- Riaz Jawoodeen for kindly editing the text;
- Shaykh Dr Jamaal Mahmood Abu Hassaan, Amman, Jordan, for kindly accepting my request to write the foreword.

May Allāh increase His bounty over them and grant them manifold reward.

Contents

Chapter Three: His Manner of Dressing & the Colours Of His Clothing

Bibliography

Sayyidunā Abū Bakr would recite this verse, on seeing *Sayyidunā Rasūlullāh* : زَايَلَهُ الظَّلَامُ كَضَوْءِ الْبَدْرِ بِالْخَيْرِ يَدْعُو أَمِيْنٌ مُصْطَفَى

"He is the faithful, chosen by Allāh, and calls for forgiveness. He shines like the full moon while it is far from darkness!"

Foreword

In the Name of Allāh, Most Gracious, Most Merciful.

All Praise is due to Allāh, Lord of the worlds. Peace and salutations upon he who was sent as a mercy to all the worlds, *Sayyidunā* Muḥammad *Rasūlullāh* , and upon his pure, righteous family, and all those who follow their path until the Day of *Qiyāmah*.

My noble brother, Mohammed Luqmaan, has honoured me, by asking me to write a few lines, as a foreword to his humble work, through which he wants to deliver a special message to our brothers in Islam. This work that he has compiled is about some of the significant traits of the noble Prophet , who Allāh has commanded us to take as our role model, just as He commanded the noble Prophet to follow those Prophets (may peace and salutations of Allāh be upon them all) who preceded him. This emulation is necessary so that the rope of Allāh can remain connected from beginning to end, in a perfect chain throughout the different eras, so that mankind can find its true humanity that has long been absent, within the exemplary personality of the noble Prophet .

How can this be possible for a human being who desires to find his true humanity and his true entity, if he does not know something important about whom he can take as a role model? Indeed, the one who traverses a certain path should not have his eyes closed, so that he does not fall into something of which the outcome is not praiseworthy. To Allāh belongs all praise, for surely, the life history of the blessed Prophet is clearer and more understandable than the life history of anyone else, for all who tread on his path.

It is an important step for my brother Mohammed Luqmaan to publish this humble work, by transmitting some significant traits and attributes of the noble *Rasūlullāh* , to our Muslim brethren, so that walking behind the noble Prophet and the noble *Sharī'ah* (Islamic Legislation) of Allāh , can be enlightening. Certainly, this work of his, even if it is a translation from an old book, is without a doubt, complex and difficult.

I ask Allāh to reward brother Luqmaan with the best of rewards, and to elevate his status in this world and the Hereafter, through the blessings of the noble Prophet , and through his sincerity.

I ask Allāh to grant him the best of luck and steadfastness. All praise is due to Allāh, Lord of the worlds.

Shaykh Dr. Jamaal Mahmood Abu Hassaan Lecturer of *'Ulum al-Qur'ān* & *Tafsīr* Amman, Jordan

A Biography on the Author Imam Muḥammad ibn 'Abd-Allāh al-Wāsiṭī al-Baghdādī Ghiyāth al-Dīn Abū

al-Makārim al-Shāfi'ī , the author of the original Arabic text, was known as Imam ibn al-'Āqūlī .

Imam ibn Qāḍī Shuhbah states about the Imam ibn al-'Āqūlī in his book, *Ṭabaqāt al-Shāfi'iyyah*: He is the heart of Iraq, the teacher of Baghdad, its scholar, as well as the heart of scholars in the east. The Imam was born in the year 733 H, during the month of *Rajab* and grew up in Baghdad. He learnt Islamic studies from his father, as well as from a group of highly learned scholars. Another group of scholars gave him permission to narrate and write about the life of the holy Prophet Muḥammad , the holy *Qur'ān*, and other academic sciences of Islam.[2]

What's more, Imam Shihāb al-Dīn ibn Ḥajar made mention of the Imam : The Imam was the teacher of all those who seeked help and knowledge in Baghdad, just like his father and grandfather. He was brilliant in the sciences of the *Ḥadīth*, its meanings and interpretations. He wrote a commentary on the book, *al-Minhaj*, by Imam al-Bayḍāwī .

Imam al-Zarkalī , in reference to the Imam , mentions the vast amount of scholarly work produced by Imam ibn al-'Āqūlī in his book, *Al-A'lām*. Some of these works are:

- *A Demonstration of what is Appropriate for Propagating Islam in the World*;
- *Al-Minhaaj: A Commentary on Imam Baghawi's book, Lamps of The Sunnah*;
- *Insight in Recognising Narrations*;

- *Adequacy of the Devotee in Recognising the Rites of Prayer*; and
- *Reports on Makkah and the City of the Beloved Messenger* .[3]

These books are clear examples of the fact that Imam ibn al-'Āqūlī was recognised as a profound scholar, respected and acknowledged for his knowledge and his contribution to Islam.

Author's Introduction "My guidance cannot come, except from Allāh."[4]

All praise is due to Allāh, the One Who sent the holy Prophet Muḥammad as a mercy to humanity, as a blessing that suffices more than the water of clouds, as a light that put to shame the glow of flowers and removed the Muslim community from darkness. Allāh is the One Who sent His Prophet as a witness over all nations. The holy Prophet delivered the message of Allāh , and is the messenger of glad tidings for what Allāh has prepared in the abode of peace. The Prophet Muḥammad came as a warner and admonished the people about the Day of Resurrection, when the hearts of humanity will be at their throats because of overwhelming astonishment. The noble Prophet invited to the path of Allāh and with The Almighty's permission sat at the table of honour, and represented an illuminating lamp free of darkness.

I praise Allāh through His guidance alone, which is from the greatest of His many blessings, and I am grateful to Allāh with gratitude that guarantees more provisions of His blessings. I bear witness that there is no one worthy of worship except Allāhalone, He has no partner, is a Deity worthy of worship in the instinct of the intellect, and is far beyond the characteristics of impurities and faults.

I bear witness that Muḥammad is His servant and Messenger, a noble Prophet that Allāh chose for inviting His creation to Islam. Peace and salutations upon *Rasūlullāh* , and upon his family and Companions, who are role models and symbols of courage, and who inspired us as ordinary people to drink knowledge from their hands. They were heroes in the depths of battle; upon them be eternal salutations that will remain as long as the name of *Rasūlullāh* is together with Allah's name in the *Adhān* (call to prayer) and the *Iqāmah* (establishment of prayer), and in the sermons and the testimony of Islam. May Allāh send abundance of peace upon them.

This is a summarized book that compiles much of the characteristics of *Rasūlullāh* , his actions, and much of his sayings. Such an endeavour requires knowledge about the Prophet r so that our belief can recall his status. The completion of this act takes place through remembering the name, the lineage, the attributes, and the actions and sayings of the *Rasūlullāh* .

With regards to the name of an individual, it forms a characteristic that provides proof about the person it refers to, and when implied, one understanding that the name refers to such a person. Allah says, "Do you know of any who is worthy of the same name as Him."[5]

In consideration of the lineage of *Rasūlullāh* , it is important because Allāh has divided the children of the Prophet Ādam into nations and tribes. Thus, Allāh states, "And We made you into nations and tribes so that you may know each other."[6]

In retrospect of the attributes of *Rasūlullāh* , they remove the traces of ignorance after defining the name and the lineage, and these attributes highlight the one, who is described, as if he is present in front of us. Hence, because the attributes are beautiful, he is loved in the centre of the heart.

What's more, the actions of *Rasūlullāh* have been witnessed by multitudes of people. Likewise, a scholar is capable of defining the Creator .

In addition, the sayings of *Rasūlullāh* are a clear definition of knowing the personality who declared them and his level of perfection. It is therefore stated, "The human being is hidden under his/her tongue."

Concerning the deeds of *Rasūlullāh* , we have not found anyone who has compiled these actions in detail before this book of ours, but rather, scholars make mention of them amongst the *ḥadīth* reports. The accounts therein prove more than the activities, except that the actions of *Rasūlullāh* increase the righteous characteristics of the holy Prophet in honour, to such an extent, which is not always highlighted by the utterances.

Indeed, *Rasūlullāh* is reported to have remaked, as narrated by Imams al-Bukhārī and Muslim , on the authority of *Sayyidah* 'Ā-ishah (may Allāh be pleased with her), "What is wrong with people that do not do as I do? By Allāh, I am the most learned of them about Allāh, and the most intense amongst them in fear of Him."

Amongst the books that compile the *Sunnah*, we have relied upon the following works:

- The compilation of Shaykh *al-'Allāmah al-Thiqah* Majd al-Dīn Mubārak ibn al-Athīr al-Jazariy , in his book, *Jāmi' al-Uṣūl*. We have narrated from him most of what we have mentioned.
- *Al-Jam'u Bayna al-Ṣaḥīḥayn*, the writing of Shaykh Ḍiyā al-Dīn Abū Ḥafṣ 'Umar ibn Badr ibn Sa'īd al-Mūṣalī ;
- The *Sunan* of Imam Abū 'Abd-Allāh Muḥammad ibn Yazīd , known as Imam ibn Mājah ;
- Amongst the expositions on the blessed qualities of *Rasūlullāh* are the following:

Dalā'il al-Nubuwwah, the writing of Imam a-Mujtahid Abū Bakr al-Bayhaqī ; and Al-Shifā, the writing of al-Qaḍī al-Sa'īd 'Iyāḍ ibn Mūsā al-Yaḥṣabī .

- Additionally, *Al-Na't*, written by Imam Abū 'Abd-Allāh Muḥammad ibn 'Alī ibn al-Ḥasan al-Ḥakīm al-Tirmidhī , and *Al-Ṭabaqāt*, by Imam Abū 'Abd-Allāh Muḥammad ibn Sa'd ibn Munī' also provide an elaboration on the qualities of *Rasūlullāh* .

These works are the origins that all scholars of this field of knowledge rely upon, and are acknowledged and received with acceptance.

Al-Ḥāfiẓ al-'Allāmah Abū al-Makārim Muḥammad ibn 'Abd-Allāh al-Wāṣiṭī al-Baghdādī Ghiyāth al-Dīn ibn al-'Āqūlī

Translator's Introduction In the Name of Allāh, The Most Gracious, The Most Merciful.

All Praise is due to Allāh, Lord of the worlds, the Creator, the One, the Eternal Absolute, He Who was not begotten nor begets, He unto Whom there is no one similar. Eternal peace and salutations upon the best of creation, the Seal of all Prophets, the mercy to all the worlds, the reason for creation, he, whose *nūr* (splendid light) is the first of creation, our beloved leader and Prophet, Muḥammad , and upon his family and Companions.

Allāh states in the holy *Qur'ān*: "Indeed, We have sent you as a witness, a bearer of glad tidings, and a warner."[7]

The following *ḥadīth* is mentioned in *Ṣaḥiḥ al--Bukhārī*, for the exegsis of the above-mentioned verse: Allāh says in the Torāh: "Oh My beloved Prophet! Verily, We have sent you as a witness over creation, as a bearer of glad tidings for those who follow, as a warner for those who oppose, and as a protection for the unlettered ones. You are My beloved servant and My Messenger . I have named you as the one who puts his complete trust in Me. You are neither impolite nor harsh-hearted, nor are you someone that causes inconvenience amongst people. You do not eliminate an evil act with another evil act, but you overlook the faults of people and forgive them. Allāh will not take you away from the life of this mortal world, until He has annulled all other forms of worship, and people will declare: "There is no one Worthy of worship, but Allāh." In this way, Allāh will open eyes that are blind, ears that are deaf and hearts that are sealed.[8]

By means of His infinite mercy and wisdom, Allāh had sent the noble Prophet to humanity. The noble Prophet is the best guide that anyone can have after Allāh . He is of such a high character and yet he was so humble. The noble Ṣaḥābah (the blessed Companions) used to teach their children about the history of the life of the noble Prophet . They noted and recorded everything concerning him, even the minutest of things. Many books have indeed, been written and compiled on the history of the life of the Noble Prophet in English.

In today's world, where the beloved of Allāh, *Rasūlullāh* is being insulted in the worst manner possible, many people are uninformed about him. We ourselves, that did not have the privilege of living with *Rasūlullāh* , and did not see him, need something to relate to.

I have therefore decided to translate *Al-Jāmi' Li Awṣāf al-Rasūl* , which was done by Imam Muḥammad ibn 'Abd-Allāh Ghiyāth al-Dīn , known as Imam ibn al-'Āqūlī. I hope Inshā-Allāh, that we will be able to understand the superiority of *Rasūlullāh* over the rest of creation. In this way, we will realise the significance of his noble names and other exceptional traits of him .

I am very grateful to Allāh for granting me the opportunity to work on this translation. I hope that this book instils in its readers the necessary recognition of the distinguished character and beauty of *Rasūlullāh* , so that they can realise the true splendour of the noble Prophet and his well-deserved status.

Mohammed Luqmaan ibn Goolam Sabier Ibn 'Abdul-Kareem Kagee

Chapter One: His Noble Names & Lineage And remember, when 'Īsā, the son of Maryam said: "Oh children of Isrā'īl, verily, I am the Messenger of Allāh to you, confirming what is in front of me of the Torāh, and a bearer of glad-tidings that a Messenger will come after me, whose name will be Aḥmad."[9]

Sayyidunā Jubayr ibn Muṭ'im narrates:

> The Messenger of Allāh said: "I have many names. I am Muḥammad, *Aḥmad*, *al-Māḥī* through whom Allāh will eradicate disbelief, *al-Ḥāshir* after whose coming mankind will be resurrected, and *al-'Āqib* after whom there is no prophet."[10]

Rasulullāh has numerous names. Imam al-Nawawī comments: Imam Abū Bakr ibn al-'Arabī al-Mālikī mentions in his commentary on al-Tirmidhī, *'Āriḍa al-Aḥwadhī fī Sharḥ al-Tirmidhī*: "Some *Ṣūfī* scholars remark: Allāh has one-thousand names and *Rasūlullāh* has one-thousand names. Regarding the names of Allāh, I have mentioned a small number of them, and with regards to the names of *Rasūlullāh* , I am aware of forty-six names."

Thereafter, Imam al-Nawawī enumerates these names and explains them in detail. Shaykh Sharf al-Dīn al-Ṭībī refers to the names of *Rasūlullāh* in his book *al-Kāshif*, which are: Muḥammad, *Aḥmad*,

Maḥmūd, al-Māḥī, al-Ḥāshir, al-'Āqib, al-Muqaffī, Nabiy al-Raḥmah, Nabiy al-Malāḥim, al-Shāhid, al-Mubash-shir, al-Nadhīr, al-Ḍaḥūk, al-Mutawakkil, al-Fātiḥ, al-Amīn, al-Muṣṭafā, al-Khātam, al-Rasūl, al-Nabiy, al-Ummiy, al-Qayyim, Nabiy al-Tawbah, al-Qāsim, al-'Abd, 'Abd-Allāh, al-Muzzammil, al-Muddath-thir, al-Shafī', al-Shāfi', al-Mushaffa', al-Ḥabīb, al-Khaṭīb, al-Ḥayyī, *al-Khalīl, al-Dā'ī, al-Sirāj al-Munīr, Ḥarīṣun 'Alaykum, Ra'ūfun Raḥīmun, al-Ṭayyib, Dhū al- 'Azm, al-Ṣāḥib, al-Ṣāliḥ, al-Sayyid, al-Qā'id, al-Imām, al-Ḥirz, al-Nūr, al-Azwar, al-Ajwad, al-Shakūr, al-Haqq al-Mubīn, al-Karīm*, al-'Aẓīm, *al-Jabbār, al-Khabīr, al-Waliy, al-Muqaddas, Ṭāhā* and *Yāsīn*.

1.1 A Commentary on These Names

- Muḥammad : He is constantly praised.

- *Aḥmad* : The Arabs heard that Allāh is sending a Prophet whose name will be Muḥammad , so they named their boys Muḥammad before the birth of the noble Prophet . Similarly, they also gave the name *Aḥmad* to male children.
- *al-Māḥī* : Allāh will eradicate disbelief through him, by clarifying the proof of its falsehood, and each time the proof appears about disbelief being falsehood; there remains nothing of its manifestation.
- *al-Ḥāshir* : Mankind will be resurrected after the Prophet's coming and after the time of his Prophethood, i.e., he is a reason for their resurrection, and they will not be resurrected until he has been sent.

- *al-'Āqib* : He succeeds in goodness those before him.
- *al-Muqaffī* : The same meaning as *al-'Āqib*, but *al-Muqaffī* denotes nobility, and the Noble Prophet has been named this due to the high honour he holds.
- *Nabiy al-Raḥmah* : From Allah's saying, "And We have not sent you, but as a Mercy to the worlds."[11]
- *Nabiy al-Malāḥim* : Rasulullah fights the disbelievers; (*Malḥamah* means war and *Malāḥim* is the plural form of the word). This factor is due to the Prophet's mercy for them, because he brings them into Islam, thereby leading them to *Jannah*.
- *al-Shāhid*: From the Qur'anic verse, "And We have come with you as a Witness over these people".[12]
- *al-Mubash-shir* and *al-Nadhīr* : From the Qur'anic verse, "A Bringer of glad-tidings and a Warner. He gives glad-tidings for good, and warns about the punishment.
- *al-Ḍaḥūk* : Due to his smiling; he was someone that constantly smiled and did not frown, and this is one of his names in the Torāh.
- *al-Mutawakkil* : He always put his trust in Allāh, depended on Him, and left all his matters to Allāh.
- *al-Fātiḥ* : He opened the doors of knowledge for his followers.
- *al-Amīn* : The noble Prophet's people gave him this title during the period of ignorance, when they had witnessed his truthfulness and trustworthiness. Sayyidah 'Ā-ishah (may

Allāh be pleased with her) replied, when asked about the character of Rasūlullāh ,

"كَانَ خُلُقُهُ الْقُرْآنَ."

"His character is the Qur'ān!"[13]

- *al-Muṣṭafā* : From *al-Iṣṭifā*, the prime of something.
- *al-Khātam* : The last of the Prophets (peace be upon them) to be sent.
- *al-Nabiy* : He taught humanity about Allāh, and brought Islam to the entire creation.
- *al-Rasūl* : The Prophet upon whom a book was revealed. Every *Rasūl* is a *Nabiy*, but not every *Nabiy* is a *Rasūl*. *Rasūlullāh* is both a *Nabiy* and a *Rasūl*.
- *al-Ummiy* : Relating to the mother of cities, Makkah, where *Rasūlullāh* was born; or because he was unlettered.
- *al-Qayyim*: *Rasūlullāh* combines all the qualities of virtuous character. He is complete in virtuous character and flawless. It also means the one who brings humanity together by instilling harmony between them and eradicating their differences.
- *Nabiy al-Tawbah* : He came with the acceptance of all repentance.
- *al-Qāsim* : He distributed the wealth of Allāh amongst His servants.
- *al-'Abd* : He was extremely disciplined, so he was given the title of *The Servant*, meaning that he is Allah's most loyal

servant.

- ‘*‘Abd-Allāh* : The Servant Of Allāh; this is a title of specification and honour, like *The House* of Allāh.
- al-Muzzammil : He said to Sayyidah Khadījah (may Allāh be pleased with her), after the first revelation: “*Cover me*”.[14]
- *al-Muddath-thir* : This name arises from the term *al-Dithār*, which means something that a person uses to cover himself/herself. In this way, we cover ourselves with the noble *Sunnah* of *Rasūlullāh* and his exemplary character.
- *al-Ḥabīb* : Allāh loves him more than He loves any of His other creation, and the love of Allāh for His servant is an indication that Allāh wants only good for that servant.
- *al-Khaṭīb* : He will address the Prophets (peace be upon them) on the Day of *Qiyāmah* (Resurrection).
- *al-Khalīl* : He is the closest friend of Allāh.
- *al-Dā’ī* : From the Qur’anic verse, “I invite to Allah through insight.”[15]
- *al-Sirāj al-Munīr* : Within his invitation is clear, complete proof of his truthfulness.
- *Ḥarīṣun ‘Alaykum* : This name means being anxious for our welfare and wanting only that which is good, thereby leading humanity to their guidance and salvation.
- *Ra’ūfun Raḥīmun* : Derived from the names of Allāh .
- *al-Ṭayyib* : From the Qur’anic verse, “Pure women are for pure men.”[16]

- *Dhū al- 'Azm* : Possessor of determination; he was commanded to follow the Prophets of this category and was given the title.
- *al-Ṣāḥib* : From the Qur'anic verse, "Your companion has not gone astray".[17]
- *al-Ṣāliḥ* : The pious one, from the greeting of the noble Prophets (peace be upon him) when *Rasūlullāh* was taken on the *Mi'rāj*, "*A warm welcome for our pious brother.*"
- *al-Sayyid* : He is the leader of creation.
- *al-Ḥirz* : The well protected, because angels always protect him.
- *al-Nūr* : From the vision of his mother, when she saw a light coming out with him, due to which the heavens and earth were illuminated.
- *al-Azhar* : From the saying of *Sayyidunā* Wāṣifah , "*Radiant and shining in colour.*"
- *al-Ajwad* : He is the most generous of people.
- *al-Shakūr* : From the noble Prophet's words, "*Should I not be a grateful servant?*" when he had stood in prayer until his feet were swollen.
- *al-Haqq al-Mubīn* : The manifest truth; from the Qur'anic verse, "Until the Truth came to them and a clear Messenger."[18]

This title is derived from two names of Allāh, as in the Qur'anic verse, "And verily, you are of great character."[19]

- *al-Karīm* : Due to his high nobility in the eyes of Allāh.
- *al-'Aẓīm* : From the Torāh: "Great for a great nation," and the Qur'anic verse, "And verily, you are of great character."[20]
- *al-Jabbār* : He always used to overpower the enemies.
- *al-Khabīr* : From Allah's words, "So ask a well-informed about Allāh."[21]
- *al-Muqaddas* : This name means that *Rasūlullāh* was pure from all sins. Amongst the titles of the Prophet is the title *al-Shams* (The sun), and some scholars of Qur'anic exegesis explain the Qur'anic verse, "Did you not see how your Lord prolongs the shadow? If He willed, He could make it stationary, but We have made the sun its guide."[22]

This verse contains the following meanings: "The shadow" refers to the darkness of disbelief; "If He willed, He could make it stationary" means that Allāh could have stopped sending the Messengers (peace be upon them), and "the sun" refers to the noble Prophet .

1.2 The Lineage of the Noble Prophet and His Prime

***Sayyidunā* 'Umar used to recite this verse in praise of *Rasulullāh* : لَوْ كُنْتَ مِنْ شَيْءٍ سِوَى الْبَشَرِ كُنْتَ الْمُضِيْءَ لَيْلَةَ الْبَدْرِ**

"If you were other than a human being, you would be the brilliant light on the night of the full moon!"

Imam al-Bukhārī , in his chapter on the coming of the noble Prophet , determines the lineage of *Rasūlullāh* as follows: He is Muḥammad ibn 'Abd-*Allāh* ibn 'Abd al-Muṭṭalib ibn Hāshim ibn 'Abdu Manāf ibn Quṣay ibn Kilāb ibn Murrah ibn Ka'b ibn Lu'ay ibn Ghālib ibn Fahr ibn Mālik ibn al-Naḍr ibn Kanānah (ibn Khuzaymah) ibn Mudrikah ibn Ilyās ibn Muḍar ibn Nizār ibn Ma'd ibn 'Adnān.

Imam al-Nawawī explains: "Until here is the consensus of the *ummah*; as for beyond this point until Ādam , the difference in opinion is strong, of which none is authentic and relied upon."

Sayyiduna Abu Hurayrah narrates: "The Messenger of Allāh said: "I have been sent in the best of generations of the children of Ādam , generation after generation, until I was born at my appointed time."[23]

Sayyidunā Wāthilah ibn al-Asqa' narrates: I heard the Messenger of Allāh saying that, "Allāh chose the Kanānah clan from the progeny of Ismā'īl, He chose the Quraysh from the Kanānah, He chose Banū Hāshim from *Quraysh*, and He chose me from Banū Hāshim."[24]

*Sayyidunā al-*Muṭṭalib ibn Abū Wadā'ah narrates that, "*Sayyidunā* al-Abbās came to *Rasūlullāh* because he had heard some news, so the noble Prophet stood up on top of the mimbar and asked: "Who am I?"

They replied, "You are the Messenger of Allāh."

The noble Prophet said: "I am Muḥammad ibn 'Abd-Allāh ibn 'Abd al-Muṭṭalib. Surely, Allāh created the creation, and He made me from the best amongst them. Thereafter, He divided them into two groups and made me from amongst the best group of them. Then He split them into tribes and made me from the best tribe amongst them. He then separated them into houses and made me from the best house amongst them and the best person amongst them."[25]

1.3 The Marriage of 'Abd-Allāh , the Son of 'Abd al-Muṭṭalib, and the Father of *Rasūlullāh* , to Āminah (Peace be upon Her), the Daughter of Wahb, and the Mother of *Rasūlullāh*

Sayyidunā Muḥammad ibn 'Alī ibn al-Ḥusayn narrated: Āminah, the daughter of Wahb, who is the son of 'Abdu Manāf, was in her uncle's room, Wahīb, who is the son of 'Abdu Manāf, the son of Zahrah. 'Abd al-Muṭṭalib ibn Hāshim ibn 'Abdu Manāf ibn Quṣay walked towards Wahb with 'Abd al-Muṭṭalib's son, 'Abd-Allāh ibn 'Abd al-Muṭṭalib, the father of *Rasūlullāh* . 'Abd-Allāh proposed to Āminah, the daughter of Wahb, and then married her. 'Abd al-Muṭṭalib asked Wahīb for his daughter's hand, Hālah, and Wahīb gave her hand in marriage to 'Abd al-Muṭṭalib.

Thus, the marriages of 'Abd al-Muṭṭalib ibn Hāshim and 'Abd-Allāh ibn 'Abd al-Muṭṭalib were conducted together. Ḥālah gave birth to *Sayyidunā* Ḥamzah ibn 'Abd al-Muṭṭalib ; and Thuwaybah, the slave girl of Abū Lahab, nursed both *Rasūlullāh* and *Sayyidunā* Hamzah . In this way, *Sayyidunā* Ḥamzah was not only the uncle of *Rasūlullāh* , but also his wet-brother through nursing."[26]

1.4 The Pregnancy of Āminah (Peace be upon Her) with *Rasūlullāh* and His Birth *Sayyidunā* Yazīd ibn 'Abd-Allāh ibn Zam'ah narrates that his aunty said: We heard that when Āminah was pregnant with *Rasūlullāh* , she used to say: "I never felt that I was pregnant with him, and I did not find the weight of pregnancy. However, I denied the absence of my menstrual cycle; perhaps it was absent and then it would return. Someone approached me, while I was half-asleep, and said: "Have you felt that you are pregnant? It was as if I was saying: "I do not know." That person replied: "Verily, you are pregnant with the leader of this *ummah* and its Prophet. That was on a Monday.[27]

Sayyidunā ibn 'Abbās narrates that Āminah bint Wahb said, I held on to him (meaning *Rasūlullāh*) and found no hardship until I gave birth to him. When I gave birth to him, a light, illuminating what is between east and west, also came out. Then he fell onto the earth, leaning on his hands, and took hold of some sand, held it in his hand, and raised his head to the heavens.[28]

Chapter Two: His Noble Descriptions & Characteristics *Sayyidunā* Hassān ibn Thābit wrote the following couplet, in praise and awe of *Rasūlullāh* : وَأَحْسَنُ مِنْكَ لَمْ تَرَ قَطُّ عَيْنِي   وَأَجْمَلُ مِنْكَ لَمْ تَلِدِ النِّسَاءُ

خُلِقْتَ مُبَرَّءًا مِنْ كُلِّ عَيْبٍ   كَأَنَّكَ خُلِقْتَ كَمَا تَشَاءُ

"Better than you my eyes have never seen, and more handsome than you no woman has given birth to! You have been created free from every defect, as if that is how you wanted to be created!"

1. *Sayyidunā* al-Ḥasan ibn 'Alī reported: I inquired from my maternal uncle, Hind ibn Abū Hālah, about the noble features of *Rasūlullāh* . He had often described the noble features of *Rasūlullāh* in detail. I felt that I should hear from him personally some of the noble features of the blessed Prophet , so that I could make this description a testimony and proof for myself. My uncle described the noble features of *Rasūlullāh* by saying:

Rasūlullāh had great qualities and attributes in him, and people also held him in high esteem. His blessed face shone like the full moon. He was slightly taller than a person of medium height, but shorter than a tall person. His blessed head was moderately large. His blessed hair was slightly twisted. If his hair became parted in the middle he left it so, otherwise he did not habitually part his hair in the middle.

Rasūlullāh had a very luminous complexion and a wide forehead. He had dense and fine hair on his eyebrows. Both eyebrows were separate and did not meet each other in the middle, and there was a vein between them that used to expand when he became angry. His nose was prominent and had a light and lustre on it. When one first looked at him, it seemed that he had a large nose; otherwise, in itself the nose was not large. His blessed beard was full and dense. The pupil of his eye was black. His cheeks were smooth and full of flesh, and his blessed mouth was moderately wide. His blessed teeth were thin and white, and the front teeth had a slight space between them.

There was a thin line of hair from his chest to his navel, and his blessed neck was beautiful and thin, like the neck of a statue that was shaved clean, and the colour was clear and shining like pure silver. All the parts of his body were of a moderate size and fully fleshed, and his blessed body was proportionately jointed. His blessed chest and stomach were in line, but his chest was broad and wide. The space between his shoulders was wide. The bones of his joints were strong and large. His body was bright and shining, and the rest of his chest and stomach had no hair. His arms, shoulders and the upper portion of his chest had hair. His forearms were long and the palms of his hands were wide. Both the palms of his hands, as well as both feet were fully fleshed. The soles of his feet were a bit deep, his feet were smooth, and because of their cleanliness and smoothness, the water did not remain there but flowed away quickly.

When he walked, he lifted his legs with vigour, leaned slightly forward and placed his feet softly on the ground. He walked with a quick pace and his steps were rather long. When he walked, it seemed as if he was descending to a lower place, and when he looked at something, he turned his whole body towards it. His blessed sight was focused longer on the ground than in the air, dignified when noticed. He would lead his Companions, and greet the one who met him first.[29]

Sayyidunā al-Ḥasan ibn 'Alī narrates that he had asked his uncle, "Describe the manner in which *Rasūlullāh* spoke."

His uncle in turn responded:

Rasūlullāh was always worried and always occupied in thought. He was never free from thought, and never rested, was silent for long, and always spoke clearly from beginning to end. He spoke concisely, where the words were less and meaning more, and would speak without curiosity or negligence. Every word was clearer than the previous one. There was neither nonsensical talk nor were there half-talks where the meaning was not complete and could not be understood. He was not short-tempered nor did he disgrace anyone.

He always greatly appreciated the blessings of Allāh even if it was minute, and did not criticise it. He did not criticise food nor did he over-praise it. He was never angry for anything materialistic, and no one would stand up to *Rasūlullāh* if he were angry. If *Rasūlullāh* objected to something for the sake of the truth, he became so angry that no one could endure it, and no one could end that anger until he changed it. If he made a gesture or pointed at something, he did it with a full hand. When he was surprised by something, he turned his hand, and when he spoke, sometimes while talking he would move his hand. He sometimes hit the palm of his right hand with the inside part of his left thumb. When he became angry with someone, he turned his blessed face away from that person, and did not pay attention to that person. When he was happy due to humility, it seemed as if he closed his eyes. His laugh was dignified with smiles, and at that moment, his blessed front teeth glittered like white shining hailstone.[30]

Sayyidunā al-Ḥasan reports: I kept this a secret from *Sayyidunā* al-Ḥusayn ibn ʻAlī for a long time. Then I related it to him, and found out that he had already made an enquiry before me. I had enquired from him about what I had asked, and found out that he had even asked my father about *Rasūlullāh's* way of entering and exiting out of the house. He did not leave out anything about the ways and manners of *Rasūlullāh* .

2. *Sayyidunā* al-Ḥusayn said, "I asked my beloved father about the manner in which *Rasūlullāh* entered the house.

He replied:

When *Rasūlullāh* entered he distributed his time into three portions. He spent a portion of his time for Allāh, a portion towards his family, and a portion for himself. He distributed his personal portion into two, one for himself and one for the people, in such a manner that the Companions who stayed close by used to visit him. Through them, he conveyed messages to the people, and did not conceal anything from them. From the history of his life, it is clear that he gave preference to people of *taqwah* (consciousness of Allāh) amongst the *ummah*. *Rasūlullāh* distributed this time according to each person's level of *taqwa*, and granted permission for everyone to do that.

Rasūlullāh divided his time according to the people's merit in religion, so from amongst them some had one requirement, some had two requirements, while others had many requirements. *Rasūlullāh* fulfilled all their requirements. He kept them occupied with things that benefited them and the entire *ummah*. When they questioned him on certain matters, he replied to them in a manner that benefited them. He would say: "Those who are present should inform the ones who are absent regarding these matters. Those people, who for some reason could not put forward their requirements, should inform me about it. Certainly, whosoever reports a need of someone who cannot do so to a leader, Allāh will keep that person steadfast on the Day of *Qiyāmah*."

Only important and beneficial matters were discussed in his gatherings.[31]

Sayyidunā al-Ḥusayn further enquired from *Sayyidunā* Alī , "Inform me about *Rasūlullāh's* exiting out of the house, what would he do?"

Sayyidunā Ali replied:

Rasūlullāh controlled his tongue and only spoke that which was necessary. He did not waste his time in useless conversations. He would instil harmony between people and not cause division amongst them. He respected and honoured the respected ones of every group, and chose a leader for them. He would warn the people and look out for them, without concealing from anyone his happiness and pleasure. He would inspect his Companions, ask people about what was happening amongst the community, improve the good, correct it, and disgrace what was repulsive and eradicate it.

He was always the same when commanding and not different. He would not be neglectful for fear that they would do that, nor did he become weary. Every situation in his hands had something good contained in it. He would not be short of the truth, and would not pass a situation to others, but would rather handle it himself. Those who followed him from amongst the people were the choicest of them, and the best of those in his eyes were the ones who gave advice to people. The highest of them in his eyes, in status, were the best of them in sharing and support.[32]

Sayyidunā al-Ḥusayn further narrates, "I asked my father about *Rasūlullāh's* manner of sitting."

He replied:

Rasūlullāh never used to sit or stand except upon being requested to do so, he would not take the homes of others as his own home, and forbid that that should be done. If he finished with the people at a gathering, he would sit until the gathering ended, would command others to adopt the same etiquette, and give all those sitting with him their fair share of attention, so that none of them would think that one is more honourable in his eyes than the other. Whoever sat with him or stood up due to a need, he was patient with such a person, until that person left him; and whoever asked of a need, he would not turn down the request except by granting that need, or a soft reply.

He became like a father to them, and they stood up with him for the truth, close to each other and preferred by him due to their *taqwā*. His meeting with his Companions was that of intelligence, modesty, patience and trust. The Companions would not raise their voices, the rights of people were not disregarded, and the errors of the gathering were not repeated. He gave them preference based on *taqwā*, revering the elderly one and having mercy on the younger, with much humility, and supported the one in need whilst having mercy on the stranger.[33]

Sayyidunā al-Ḥasan narrates further, "I then enquired from my beloved father about *Rasūlullāh's* life amongst those who sat with him."

He replied by explicating as follows:

Rasūlullāh was always happy and easy mannered. There was always a smile and a sign of happiness on his blessed face. He was soft natured, and when his approval was needed he easily gave consent. He did not speak in a harsh tone nor was he hard-hearted. He did not scream while speaking, nor was he rude, nor did he speak indecently. He did not seek the faults of others, and never over-praised anything. He did not exceed in joking, nor was he a miser. He kept away from undesirable language and did not make as if he did not hear anything.

He completely kept himself away from three things: Arguments, pride, and senseless talks. He prohibited people from three things: He did not disgrace or insult anyone, nor look for the faults of others or expose their faults, and only spoke for that from which he could attain reward. When he spoke, those present bowed their heads in such a manner, as if birds were sitting on top, and when he completed what he wanted to say, the others would begin speaking. They did not argue with him regarding anything, and whenever someone spoke to *Rasūlullāh* , the others would keep quiet and listen until that person was finished. The speech of every person was as if the first person was speaking.

When everyone laughed for something, *Rasūlullāh* would also laugh, and when the Companions were surprised by something, he showed his surprise regarding that thing. *Rasūlullāh* exercised patience at the harshness and indecent questions of a traveller, and would say: "When you see a person in need, then always assist that person."

If someone praised him out of thanks, he would remain silent. *Rasūlullāh* did not interrupt someone talking and did not begin speaking while someone else was busy speaking. If someone exceeded the limits, *Rasūlullāh* would stop or would get up and leave."

It is also narrated that, "*Sayyidunā* al-Ḥasan queried: "Describe to me the manner of *Rasūlullāh's* silence."

Sayyiduna Ali responded:

His silence was due to four things: Forbearance, insight, considerateness, and meditation. He was considerate with respect to the fact that he took note of everyone in the gathering and listened to them with equal attention.

His meditation was for the temporary mortal life of this world and the eternal permanent life of the Hereafter.

He always combined forbearance with patience, and this is why nothing could enrage him to the extent of him losing his temper.

His insight embraced the following four things:

- He adopted good things so that others could follow him.
- He would abstain from repulsive things so that others could emulate him.
- He always deliberated on such matters that were beneficial for his *ummah*; and
- He would direct his efforts to such matters that the *ummah* could prosper from in this world and the Hereafter."[34]

3. *Sayyidunā* Muqātil ibn Ḥayyān narrates on the authority of *Sayyidunā* 'Abd-Allāh ibn al-Ḥasan , who reported from his father, that *Rasūlullāh* said: Allāh, the Highest, revealed to Prophet 'Īsa : "Oh 'Īsa ! Be serious in matters concerning Me and do not joke about them. Listen to Me and obey My commands. Oh, son of the pure virgin! You are, undoubtedly, without defects and I created you as a sign for the world, so serve Me, and put your trust in me.

Go to the people of Sūrān in Siryāniyyah, and deliver to them the message that is in front of you, that: I am Allāh, the Ever-Living, the Ever-Lasting, and the One that does not disappear.

Believe in the Unlettered Messenger, companion of the camel and the turban, the two sandals and the staff. His hair is neither very curly, nor very straight, but it is slightly wavy. His cheeks are wide, his eyebrows are separate, his eyes are big and black, its colour is like the moon, and his nose is prominent. His beard is full and dense; his neck resembles a silver jug, as if gold is lining the bones in his neck. He has hair running like a thin line from his upper chest to his navel, and does not have any other hair on his chest or stomach. The palms of his hands and his feet are fully fleshed, and his fingers and toes are moderately long.

When he walks, his walk is as if he is descending from a slope. He is a companion of few offspring, indeed his offspring is from the blessed one, *Sayyidah* Khadījah (may Allāh be pleased with her), and she has a house in the *Jannah* made of pearls, wherein there is no weariness or old age. He will be looked after near the end of time as Prophet Zakariyyā looked after your mother.

He will have from *Sayyidah* Khadījah (may Allāh be pleased with her), his daughter *Sayyidah* Fāṭimah (may Allāh be pleased with her), from whom will be born to him two happy martyrs, *Sayyidunā* al-Ḥasan and *Sayyidunā* al-Ḥusayn .

His message is al-Qur'ān, and his religion is al-Islām; *Ṭūbā* is the reward of those who lived during his days and followed his message."

Prophet 'Īsa asked, "What is *Ṭūbā?*"

Allāh replied:

"A tree in the *Jannah* that I planted on My own. Its origin is from My pleasure, its water is from *Tasnīm*, it is as cool as camphor, its taste is like that of ginger, and its smell is of musk."

Prophet 'Īsa replied: "Oh my Lord, grant me to drink from it."

Allāh responded:

"It is *ḥarām* (unlawful) for the Prophets to taste from it until the Unlettered Messenger drinks from it, and it is *ḥarām* for anyone else to drink from it until the *ummah* of that noble Prophet drinks from it."[35]

4. *Sayyidunā* 'Abd-Allāh ibn Salām said, "The attributes of *Sayyidunā* Muḥammad *Rasūlullāh* are mentioned in the Torāh. It is also mentioned therein that *Sayyidunā* 'Īsa will be buried next to *Sayyidunā* Muḥammad ."

Sayyidunā Abū Mardūod al-Madanī said in reply to this, "In the blessed chamber there has remained a place for one more grave."[36]

2.1 The Attributes of the Blessed Hair of *Rasūlullāh* 1.

Sayyidunā Qatādah relates: I asked *Sayyidunā* Anas about the blessed hair of *Rasūlullāh* , and he replied: "His hair was of two different types, neither very curly nor very straight. It was not very twisted nor very wavy, and it used to hang down until between his shoulders and his ear-lobes."

It is also narrated that, "His hair touched his shoulders."[37]

2. *Sayyidunā* ibn 'Abbās is reported to have said: The noble Prophet used to do as the People of the Book did, in matters in which there was no command from Allāh. The People of the Book used to let their hair hang down while the idolaters used to part their hair. *Rasūlullāh* did the same, and later on he parted his hair.[38]

3. Sayyidah Umm Hānī (may Allāh be pleased with her) reports that, "When *Rasūlullāh* came to Makkah after the *Hijrah*, his blessed hair had four plaits."[39]

4. *Sayyidunā* Anas said: *Rasūlullāh* disliked that a man should pluck white hair from his head and beard. *Rasūlullāh* did not dye his hair. Indeed. the whiteness of the hair was in his upper chin, in his temple hair, and on his blessed head.[40]

5. *Sayyidunā* Abū Juḥayfah said, "I saw *Rasūlullāh* , and I saw white hair under his bottom lip."[41]

6. *Sayyidunā* ibn 'Umar said, "*Rasūlullāh* had about twenty strands of white hair."[42]

7. *Sayyidunā* Jābir ibn Samurah said, when asked about the white hair of *Rasūlullāh* , "When *Rasūlullāh* oiled his hair, the white hair did not show. When he did not oil it, the white hair showed."

8. *Sayyidunā* Anas said, "I saw *Rasūlullāh* while the barber was cutting his blessed hair. His Companions were circling him, not wanting a single strand of his blessed hair to fall on the floor, but rather in one of their hands."

9. *Sayyidunā* Muḥammad ibn Sīrīn said to *Sayyidunā* ‘Ubaydah , “We have hair from the Prophet that we received from *Sayyidunā* Anas , or from the family of *Sayyidunā* Anas .”

Sayyidunā ‘Ubaydah replied, “For a hair of his to be with me is dearer to me than this world and what it contains.”43

2.2 The Blessed Face of *Rasūlullāh*

1. *Sayyidunā* al-Barrā said, “*Rasūlullāh* is the most beautiful of people in his facial features, and the best of them in creation.”44

2. *Sayyidunā* Sa’īd al-Jarīrī said, “I said to Abū al-Ṭufayl: “Did you see *Rasūlullāh* ?”

He replied: “Yes, he is brilliantly fair in complexion and very handsome.”

3. *Sayyidunā* Jābir ibn Samurah was questioned about the face of *Rasūlullāh* , “Was his blessed face shining like a sword?”

He replied, “No, but like the sun and moon with its roundness.”

4. *Sayyidunā* Anas said, "*Rasūlullāh* was radiant in colour, as if his sweat was pearls, and if he walked, he would be at complete ease. I never touched a silk garment, nor any silk softer than the palm of the hand of *Rasūlullāh* .”

Sayyidah ‘Ā-ishah (may Allāh be pleased with her) recited this verse once, when *Rasūlullāh* was with her, "وَإِذَا نَظَرْتَ إِلَى أَسِرَّةِ وَجْهِهِ كَبَرْقِ الْعَارِضِ الْمُتَهَلِّلِ."بَرَقَتْ

“If you watch his face, you will see it twinkling like the lightning of an approaching rain!”

2.3 The Blessed Mouth of *Rasūlullāh* *Sayyidunā* Jābir ibn Samurah said, "*Rasūlullāh* had a wide mouth. There were red lines in the whiteness of his eyes. He had little flesh on his heels and had big feet."

2.4 The Attributes of the Speech of *Rasūlullāh* 1. *Sayyidah* 'Ā-ishah (may Allāh be pleased with her) narrates that, "The speech of the noble Prophet was not quick and continuous. He spoke clearly, word for word. A person sitting in his company remembered what he said."

2. *Sayyidunā* Anas narrates that the Prophet used to repeat words three times so that you could think about what he said.

3. *Sayyidah* 'Ā-ishah (may Allāh be pleased with her) said, "The speech of *Rasūlullāh* was not quick and continuous. Everyone who heard his words understood him."

4. *Sayyidunā* 'Abd-Allāh ibn Salām said that, "When *Rasūlullāh* sat down to talk, he would constantly raise his eyesight to the sky."

5. *Sayyidunā* Mus'ir reports, "I heard an elderly man in the mosque saying: "I heard Jābir ibn 'Abd-Allāh saying: "Within the speech of *Rasūlullāh* there was slow recitation or chanting."

2.5 The Blessed Voice of *Rasūlullāh* *Sayyidunā* Anas said: Allāh did not send a Prophet before *Rasūlullāh* , except that he was very handsome and had a melodious voice. Your noble Prophet is the most handsome amongst all of them, and has the most melodious voice.

2.6 The Length of the Index-Finger of *Rasūlullāh*

Sayyidah Maymūnah bint Kardam (may Allāh be pleased with her) said: I performed the pilgrimage with *Rasūlullāh* , and I saw *Rasūlullāh* on his camel. My father went to ask him something. I indeed, found myself, amazed at the length of his blessed index finger that followed his thumb, compared to the rest of his fingers.

2.7 The Seal of Prophethood 1. *Sayyidunā* 'Abd-Allāh ibn Sarjas said: I saw *Rasūlullāh* and ate a meal of bread and meat with him. After the meal, I told him: "Oh *Rasūlullāh* ! May Allāh forgive you."

He replied: "And you too."

The narrator then enquired: "Should I ask forgiveness for you, Oh *Rasūlullāh* ?"

The Prophet replied, "Yes, and for yourself."

Then he recited the words of Allāh : "And ask forgiveness for your sins, and for the believing men and believing women."

The narrator reports further, "Then I stood behind him and looked at the Seal of Prophethood between his shoulders, located at the upper portion of his left shoulder. On it were moles that resembled beauty spots."

2. *Sayyidunā* Jābir ibn Samurah reports that, "The Seal of Prophethood of *Rasūlullāh* , located between his two shoulders, resembled a red tumour (protruding flesh), and was equivalent to the size of a pigeon's egg."

2.8 The Walking of *Rasūlullāh* 1. *Sayyidunā* Abū Hurayrah said, "I never saw something better than *Rasūlullāh* in his walk; it is as if the sun was moving in his face."

He also said, "I never saw anyone faster than *Rasūlullāh* in his walk; it is as if the earth was contained for him. If we walked with him, we used to strain ourselves, while he would be at full ease."

2. *Sayyidunā* Anas said, "When the Prophet walked, he used to take a rest."

2.9 The Shadow of *Rasūlullāh* *Sayyidunā* Dhakwān narrates that, "*Rasūlullāh* was never seen with a shadow in the sunlight nor under moon light, and no traces were seen after he had relieved himself."

2.10 The Frangrance of the Pure Scent of *Rasūlullāh* *Sayyidunā* Anas said, "I never smelt a scent before, nor a pure smell, better than the scent of *Rasulullah* ."

2.11 The Sweat, the Blood, and the Bodily Matter of *Rasūlullāh* 1. *Sayyidunā* Anas said, "*Rasulullah* entered

our house and slept there, and he was sweating. My mother came in with a glass and began to collect the sweat in it. The Prophet woke up and said, “Oh Umm Salīm, what are you doing?”

She replied, “This is your sweat that we are collecting for our medicine, because your sweat is the purest of medicine.”

2. *Sayyidunā* Mālik ibn Sinān narrates that he drank the blood of *Rasūlullāh* , and *Rasūlullāh* permitted it, and said, “The Fire will never touch him.”

3. *Sayyidah* ‘Ā-ishah (may Allāh be pleased with her) said, "*Rasūlullāh* used to enter the bathroom to relieve himself, and when he came out, I entered. I was received by the scent of musk and did not see any traces there. I therefore said to him, "When you enter the place to relieve yourself, and come out from it and I enter, a scent of musk receives me, and I do not see any traces.”

He replied, “Undoubtedly, us, the congregation of Prophets, our bodies have been created from the souls of *Jannah*, and whenever we relieve ourselves, the earth swallows it.”

Chapter Three: His Manner of Dressing & the Colours Of His Clothing

3.1 The White Colour of His Clothes *Sayyidunā* ibn Shihāb narrates the following event: *Sayyidunā* ‘Urwah ibn Zubayr informed me that Rasulullāh met *Sayyidunā*

Zubayr amongst a group of Muslims that were businessmen returning from *Shām* (Syria), *Sayyidunā* Zubayr covered *Sayyidunā Rasūlullāh* and *Sayyidunā* Abū Bakr with a white garment. When the Muslims in *al-Madīnah* heard about *Rasūlullāh's* migration from Makkah they would go out every morning in the heat, and wait for him until the heat of the afternoon caused them to return indoors.

Hence, one day they turned around after they had prolonged their waiting, and when they returned to their homes, a Jewish man climbed on top of one of their fortresses to see something. He saw *Rasūlullāh* and his Companions dressed in white, looking beautiful to such an extent that the rainbow would disappear.The Jewish man did nothing, but proclaim with a loud voice: "Oh groups of Arabs! your leader that you are awaiting approaches."

3.2 The Black Colour of His Clothes *Sayyidunā* 'Amr ibn Ḥarīth said, "I saw the Prophet , and on him was a black turban, which ended between his shoulders."

3.3 The Red Garb *Sayyidunā* al-Barrā said, "*Rasūlullāh* had a wide space between his shoulders, and he had hair that reached the bottom tip of his ear. I saw him in a red garb, and never saw something more handsome than him before."

3.4 The Yellow Garb 1. *Sayyidunā* 'Abd-Allāh ibn Ja'far said, "I saw *Rasūlullāh* and on him were a garb and a turban, both dyed with saffron."

2. *Sayyidunā* Yaḥyā ibn 'Abd-Allāh ibn Mālik narrates that, "*Rasūlullāh* used to dye his clothes with saffron; *i.e.* his shirt, garb and turban."[45]

3. *Sayyidunā* 'Abd-Allāh ibn 'Amr ibn al-'Ās narrates that: *Rasūlullāh* saw me wearing two garments dyed with safflower, and he asked: "Did your mother tell you to do this?"

I, in turn enquired from him: "Must I wash it, Oh *Rasūlullāh* ?"

He replied: "No, but rather burn it."

4. In another narration, *Rasūlullāh* said, "Surely, this kind of garment is from the clothing of the disbelievers, so do not wear it."

In another narration, *Rasūlullāh* said, "Dispose of it."

Sayyidunā 'Abd-Allāh ibn 'Amr asked, "Where, Oh *Rasūlullāh* ?" He replied, "In a fire."

3.5 The Green Scarf *Sayyidunā* Abū Rimthah said, "I saw *Rasūlullāh* wearing two green scarves."

3.6 His Scarf *Sayyidunā* Anas said, "The most dearest of clothes to the Prophet to wear was the scarf."

3.7 His *Qamīṣ* (*Thowb*) 1. *Sayyidah* Umm Salamah (may Allāh be pleased with her) stated, "The most dearest of clothes to *Rasūlullāh* was the *qamīṣ* (*thowb*)."

2. *Sayyidunā* Anas said, "The *qamīṣ* of *Rasūlullāh* was made of cotton, it was short in length, and had a short collar."

3.8 His *Jubbah* 1. *Sayyidunā* 'Abd-Allāh , the friend of *Sayyidah* Asmā (may Allāh be pleased with her) remarked, Asmā took out a *Jubbah* for us that was used to cover the head and shoulders. She said: "This is the *Jubbah* of *Rasūlullāh* that was with *Sayyidah* 'Ā-ishah (may Allāh be pleased with her), and when she passed away I took it. We wash it for a sick person when he complains of pain."

2. *Sayyidunā* 'Umar said, "I saw Abū al-Qāsim wearing a *Jubbah* from *Shām*, which had a narrow collar."

3.9 The Cloak of *Rasulullāh* *Sayyidunā* 'Urwah ibn al-Zubayr narrates that the clothing and the cloak of the Prophet , which he used to don in delegations, were from Ḥadramowt. These garments were the length of four arms, and the width of two arms and one hand.[46]

3.10 His Waist-Wrap 1. *Sayyidunā* Abū Burdah said, "I entered the house of *Sayyidah* 'Ā-ishah (may Allāh be pleased with her), and she took out for us a matted garment and a dark waist-wrap, which were both made in Yemen."

Sayyidunā Abū Burdah said, "I take an oath by Allah: Verily, *Rasūlullāh* passed away in these two pieces of clothing."

2. *Sayyidunā* Sahl ibn Sa'd said: A woman came to the Prophet with a scarf that she wove on her own. She said to him: "Oh *Rasūlullāh* ! I wove this scarf with my hands and present it to you, hoping that you will wear it."

Sayyidunā Sahl said: "*Rasūlullāh* took the scarf because he liked it, and came to meet us with the scarf on his blessed head. A man amongst the people saw it and exclaimed: "Oh *Rasūlullāh* , how beautiful is this scarf! Please allow me to wear it."

Rasūlullāh replied: "Certainly."

Then *Rasūlullāh* r sat in the gathering as long as Allāh allowed him and then went back inside. After *Rasūlullāh* entered, he folded it, and then sent it to the man. As a result, the people reprimanded that man by saying: “You have not acted in a good manner. *Rasūlullāh* wore the scarf because he needed it, and then you asked him for it, as you knew that he would not refuse someone who asks.”

The man replied, “By Allāh, I have not asked him for it so that I can wear it, but I asked him for it so that it could be my *kafan* (shroud) on the day I die.”

Sayyidunā Sahl narrates: “As a result, it became the *kafan* of that man.”

3. *Sayyidunā* Yazīd ibn Abū Ḥabīb narrates that *Rasūlullāh* used to open the scarf in front of him, and lift it from behind him.

3.11 The Prophet Once Wore a Silk Garment 1. *Sayyidunā* Maysūr ibn Mukhrimah declared: Rasulullah divided some outer garments amongst us and did not give Mukhrimah anything. Mukhrimah, the father of *Sayyidunā* Maysūr, told him: “Oh my son, come with us to *Rasūlullāh* .”

I thus went with him, and he said to me: “Go inside and call *Rasūlullāh* for me."

I did so on the request of my father. When Rasulullah came out, he had an outer garment on, and he said to Mukhrimah: “We hid this away for you.”

Mukhrimah looked at it and was pleased. In another narration, it is mentioned that, “*Rasūlullāh* came out wearing a silk garment that had gold buttons."

2. *Sayyidunā* 'Uqbah ibn 'Āmir said: A silk garment was presented as a gift to *Rasūlullāh* . He wore it, performed *ṣalāh* while wearing the garment and then left. Then he removed it forcefully, like someone who hated it, and exclaimed: "This is not suitable for those who are conscious of Allah."

3.12 Wearing New Clothing on a Friday 1. *Sayyidunā* Anas said, "If *Rasūlullāh* had new clothes, he would wear it on a Friday."

2. *Sayyidunā* Abū Sa'īd said: When *Rasūlullāh* had new clothes, he called it by its name, for *e.g.* a turban, or a *qamīṣ*, or a garment. Then he would recite: "Oh Allāh, to You belongs the praise for dressing me in this. I ask You for its good and the good of what it was made for, and I seek refuge in You from its evil and from the evil for what it was made."

3.13 The Leather Socks 1. *Sayyidunā* Buraydah narrates that al-Najāshī gave *Rasūlullāh* as a gift a pair of simple leather socks, which he wore."

"Oh you enveloped in garments! Arise and warn! Moreover, magnify your Lord! And purify your clothes!"[47]

3.14 The Ring 1. *Sayyidunā* Anas narrates that he saw a ring made of silver one day on the hand of *Rasūlullāh* . Then the people made rings from silver

and began to wear them. When *Rasūlullāh* disposed of his ring, the people did likewise.

2. *Sayyidunā* Ibn 'Umar narrates that *Rasūlullāh* made a ring from gold, and he would place its lobe in the centre of his hand-palm when he wore it. Consequently, the people did the same. Then, *Rasūlullāh* sat on top of the mimbar, removed the ring and said: "I used to wear this ring and place its lobe from the inside of my hand." Then he threw the ring and said, "By Allāh, I will not wear it ever again."

اَللّٰهُمَّ صَلِّ عَلٰى بَدْرِ التَّمَامِ

اَللّٰهُمَّ صَلِّ عَلٰى نُوْرِ الظَّلَامِ

اَللّٰهُمَّ صَلِّ عَلٰى مِفْتَاحِ دَارِ السَّلَامِ

اَللّٰهُمَّ صَلِّ عَلٰى الشَّفِيْعِ فِيْ جَمِيْعِ الْأَنَامِ

"Oh Allah, Send salutations upon the full moon of perfection! Send salutations upon the light of all darkness! Send salutations upon the key to the Abode of Peace! Send salutations upon the intercessor for the entire creation!"

Bibliography

Al-'Asqalānī, Aḥmad ibn Ḥajar. *Fatḥ al-Bārī: Sharḥ Ṣaḥīḥ al-Bukhārī*. Riyadh: Dar al-Salam, 2000.

Al-Nawawī, Yaḥyā ibn Sharf. *Ṣaḥīḥ Muslim bi Sharḥ al-Nawawī*. Cairo: Maktabah al-Iman.

Al-Qazwīnī, Abū ‘Abd-Allāh ibn Mājah. *Sunan ibn Mājah*. Riyadh: Bayt al-Afkar al-Dauliyyah.

Al-Sijistānī, Muḥammad ibn Sulaymān ibn al-Ash’ath. *Sunan Abī Dāwūd*. Riyadh: Bayt al-Afkar al-dauliyyah.

Al-Tirmidhī, Muḥammad ibn ‘Īsā ibn Sowrah. *Al-Shamā’il al-Muḥammadiyyah*. Beirut: Dar Ihya al-Turath al-‘Arabiy.

Al-Tirmidhī, Muḥammad ibn ‘Īsā ibn Sowrah. *Jāmi’ al-Tirmidhī*. Riyadh: Bayt al-Afkar al-Dauliyyah, 2004.

Al-Zarkalī, Khayr al-Dīn. *Al-A’lām*. Accessed on 03 June 2020. URL: http://shamela.ws/index.php/book/12286.

Al-Zuhriy, Muḥammad ibn Sa’d ibn Munī’. *Al-Ṭabaqāt al-Kubrā*. Beirut: Dar Iḥya al-Turath al-‘Arabiy.

Ibn al-‘Āqūlī, Ghiyāth al-Dīn. *Al-Jāmi’ li Awṣāf al-Rasūl*. Cairo: Al-Maktab al-Thaqāfiy li al-Nashr wa al-Towzi’, 2002).

Ibn Thābit, Ḥassān. *Diwān Ḥassān ibn Thābit*. Beirut: Dar al-Kutub al-‘Ilmiyyah, 2002.

Shuhbah, Taqiy al-Dīn ibn Qāḍī. *Ṭabaqāt al-Shāfi’iyyah*. Accessed on 03 June 2020. URL: http://shamela.ws/index.php/book/6736.

The Holy *Qur’ān*. Damascus: Dar ‘Ulum al-Qur’an, 2005.

Notes

[←1]

Ḥassān ibn Thābit, *Diwān Ḥassān ibn Thābit* (Beirut: Dar al-Kutub al-‘Ilmiyyah, 2002), 66.

[←2]

Taqiy al-Dīn ibn Qāḍī Shuhbah, *Ṭabaqāt al-Shāfi'iyyah*, Volume 3, 177, http://shamela.ws/index.php/book/6736.

[⟵3]

Khayr al-Dīn al-Zarkalī, *Al-A'lām*, Volume 7, 43, http://shamela.ws/index.php/book/12286.

[←4]

The Holy *Qur'ān* (Damascus: Dar 'Ulum al-Qur'an, 2005), *Sūrah Hūd*, 11: 88.

[←5]

The Holy *Qur'ān*, *Sūrah Maryam*, 19: 65.

[←6]

The Holy *Qur'ān*, *Sūrah al-Hujurāt*, 49: 13.

[←7]

The Holy *Qur'ān, Sūrah al-Fatḥ*. 48: 8.

[←8]

Aḥmad ibn Ḥajar al-'Asqalānī, *Fatḥ al-Bārī: Sharḥ Ṣaḥīḥ al-Bukhārī* (Riyadh: Dar al-Salam, 2000), Volume 8, 744.

[←9]

The Holy *Qur'ān*, *Sūrah al-Ṣaff*, 61: 6.

[←10]

Aḥmad ibn Ḥajar al-'Asqalānī, *Fatḥ al-Bārī: Sharḥ Ṣaḥīḥ al-Bukhārī*, Volume 6, 678.

[←11]

The Holy *Qur'ān, Sūrah al-Ambiyā'*, 21: 107.

[←12]

The Holy *Qur'ān, Sūrah al-Nisā'*, 4: 41.

[←13]

Aḥmad Ibn Ḥajar al-'Asqalānī, Fatḥ al-Bārī: Sharḥ Ṣaḥīḥ al-Bukhārī (Riyadh: Dar al-Salam, 2000), Volume 6. 575.

[←14]

Aḥmad Ibn Ḥajar al-'Asqalānī, *Fatḥ al-Bārī: Sharḥ Ṣaḥīḥ al-Bukhārī*, Volume 1, 30.

[←15]

The Holy *Qur'ān*, *Sūrah Yūsuf*, 12: 108.

[←16]

The Holy *Qur'ān*, *Sūrah al-Nūr*, 24: 26.

[←17]

The Holy *Qur'ān*, *Sūrah al-Najm*, 53: 2.

[←18]

The Holy *Qur'ān*, *Sūrah al-Zukhruf*, 43: 29.

[←19]

The Holy *Qur'ān, Sūrah al-Qalam,* 68: 4.

[←20]

The Holy *Qur'ān, Sūrah al-Qalam,* 68: 4.

[←21]

The Holy *Qur'ān*, *Sūrah al-Furqān*, 25: 59.

[←22]

The Holy *Qur'ān, Sūrah al-Furqān*, 25: 45.

[←23]

Aḥmad Ibn Ḥajar al-‘Asqalānī, *Fatḥ al-Bārī: Sharḥ Ṣaḥīḥ al-Bukhārī*, Volume 6, 691.

[←24]

Yaḥyā ibn Sharf al-Nawawī, *Ṣaḥīḥ Muslim bi Sharḥ al-Nawawī* (Cairo: Maktabah al-Iman), Volume 8, 33.

[←25]

Muḥammad ibn 'Īsā ibn Sowrah al-Tirmidhī, *Jāmi' al-Tirmidhī* (Riyadh: Bayt al-Afkar al-Dauliyyah, 2004), 567.

[←26]

Muḥammad ibn Sa’d ibn Munī’ al-Zuhriy, *al-Ṭabaqāt al-Kubrā* (Beirut: Dar Iḥya al-Turath al-‘Arabiy), Volume 1, 44.

[←27]

Muḥammad ibn Sa’d ibn Munī’ al-Zuhriy, *al-Ṭabaqāt al-Kubrā*, Volume 1, 45.

[←28]

Muḥammad ibn Sa'd ibn Munī' al-Zuhriy, *al-Ṭabaqāt al-Kubrā*, Volume 1, 45.

[←29]

Muḥammad ibn ‘Īsā ibn Sowrah al-Tirmidhī, *Al-Shamā’il al-Muḥammadiyyah* (Beirut: Dar Ihya al-Turath al-‘Arabiy), 20.

[←30]

Muḥammad ibn ʻĪsā ibn Sowrah al-Tirmidhī, *Al-Shamā'il al-Muḥammadiyyah*, 21.

[←31]

Muḥammad ibn ʻĪsā ibn Sowrah al-Tirmidhī, *Al-Shamā'il al-Muḥammadiyyah*, 21.

[←32]

Muḥammad ibn ʻĪsā ibn Sowrah al-Tirmidhī, *Al-Shamā'il al-Muḥammadiyyah*, 22.

[←33]

Muḥammad ibn ʻĪsā ibn Sowrah al-Tirmidhī, *Al-Shamā'il al-Muḥammadiyyah*, 22.

[←34]

Muḥammad ibn ʻĪsā ibn Sowrah al-Tirmidhī, *Al-Shamā'il al-Muḥammadiyyah*, 23.

[←35]

Ghiyāth al-Dīn ibn al-'Āqūlī, *Al-Jāmi' li Awṣāf al-Rasūl* (Cairo: Al-Maktab al-Thaqāfiy li al-Nashr wa al-Towzi', 2002), 66.

[←36]

Muḥammad ibn ʻĪsā ibn Sowrah al-Tirmidhī, *Jāmi' al-Tirmidhī*,

[←37]

Aḥmad Ibn Ḥajar al-‘Asqalānī, *Fatḥ al-Bārī: Sharḥ Ṣaḥīḥ al-Bukhārī*, Volume 10, 437.

[←38]

Aḥmad Ibn Ḥajar al-‘Asqalānī, *Fatḥ al-Bārī: Sharḥ Ṣaḥīḥ al-Bukhārī*, Volume 10, 443.

[←39]

Muḥammad ibn Sulaymān ibn al-Ash'ath al-Sijistānī, *Sunan Abī Dāwūd* (Riyadh: Bayt al-Afkar al-dauliyyah), 457.

[←40]

Yaḥyā ibn Sharf al-Nawawī, *Ṣaḥīḥ Muslim bi Sharḥ al-Nawawī*, Volume 8, 33.

[←41]

Aḥmad Ibn Ḥajar al-‘Asqalānī, *Fatḥ al-Bārī: Sharḥ Ṣaḥīḥ al-Bukhārī*, Volume 6, 689.

[←42]

Abū ʻAbd-Allāh ibn Mājah al-Qazwīnī, *Sunan ibn Mājah* (Riyadh: Bayt al-Afkar al-Dauliyyah), 391.

[←43]

Aḥmad Ibn Ḥajar al-‘Asqalānī, *Fatḥ al-Bārī: Sharḥ Ṣaḥīḥ al-Bukhārī*, Volume 1, 358.

[←44]

Aḥmad Ibn Ḥajar al-‘Asqalānī, *Fatḥ al-Bārī: Sharḥ Ṣaḥīḥ al-Bukhārī*, Volume 6, 690.

[←45]

Muḥammad ibn Sa’d ibn Munī’ al-Zuhriy, *al-Ṭabaqāt al-Kubrā*, Volume 1, 452.

[←46]

Muḥammad ibn Sa'd ibn Munī' al-Zuhriy, *al-Ṭabaqāt al-Kubrā*, Volume 1, 45.

[←47]

The holy Qur'ān, *Sūrah* al-*Muddath-thir*, 74: 1-4.

www.ingramcontent.com/pod-product-compliance
Lightning Source LLC
Chambersburg PA
CBHW070643030426
42337CB00020B/4146
9780639784663